Life After The Field

LIFE AFTER THE FIELD

Benjamin Martin

Copyright © 2021 by Benjamin L. Martin

All rights reserved. No part of this book may be reproduced or used in any manner without written permission of the copyright owner except for the use of quotations in a book review.

First paperback edition March 2021

Book design by Benjamin L Martin

ISBN 978-0-5788-4074-1 (paperback)

ISBN 978-0-5788-4075-8 (e-book)

Published by Martin Etiquettes LLC

Life After The Field

Table of Contents

Dedication
Chapter 1: Introduction
Chapter 2: An Explanation to Consider
Chapter 3: Finding the New You
Chapter 4: The Search for New Passion
Chapter 5: Learning the Basics
Chapter 6: Mastering the Craft
Chapter 7: The Devil Is in the Routine
Chapter 8: Diversify Your Skill Set
Chapter 9: Mind Control
Chapter 10: Execution
A Letter to Former Athletes
About the Author

Life After The Field

Dedication

This book is dedicated to the former athlete that lays awake at night anxious for more but has no idea where to look.

This book is dedicated to anyone passing from one stage of life to another and needs a guide.

This book is dedicated to those who suffer from the depression of trying to fill a void that consistently leaves you empty and confused.

This book is dedicated to all athletes looking for a new beginning.

This book is dedicated to my family for showing me that I'm always more than I could ever imagine.

Life After The Field

Chapter 1: The Introduction

"Retiring was my final victory. Not staying a minute too long, or a season too long, let me leave on my own terms. Knowing when to retire is difficult for any athlete or businessperson. You have to give up so much and start another life. But making that decision and sticking to it is one of the most rewarding decisions you will ever make in your life. I encourage people to look at this moment as starting a new season in a different game".

- Bill Russell

Life After The Field

I remember it as if it happened yesterday. At the 2016 Track & Field NCAA Regional Championships in Jacksonville, Florida, I ran the last 100-meter sprint I'd ever run for the rest of my life. After I grabbed my things, I went alone to watch the rest of the track meet as a beautiful sunset bathed the stadium. It was somewhat a poetic and symbolic ending to my career. My initial feeling was that of relief and pleasure; having completed 17 years of competitive athletics, I felt like suddenly the weight of constant workouts, the pressure to perform, and task overload finally had ended. After about a few months to half a year of adjusting to life outside of athletics, I discovered a new feeling. There was this nagging urge to prepare for something, weird anxiety to want to achieve another goal, reach another milestone or attack a new challenge. To my disappointment I couldn't find anything that would properly fill the crater sized void a lifetime of athletics had left. Then it hit me, I'd undergone my first death.

Hello. My name is Ben Martin. I'm a retired multi-sport athlete with experience in baseball, football, and basketball annually since the age of 5. Around high school, I dropped basketball and focused solely on football and baseball. After a trial

Life After The Field

period recommended by my father, I fell in love with track & field, where I'd go on to become a High School State Champion in two events and sign a NCAA Division 1 scholarship with Troy University. Through my five-year collegiate career at Troy I'd finish as a Two-Time Sun Belt Conference Champion, Two-Time NCAA Academic All American and School Record Holder for the 100 Meter Dash, and that's only the more notable accomplishments. I like to make this distinctive introduction of myself not to brag but to establish my credibility as a former athlete who understands where you're coming from. I understand the level of dedication, diligence, and energy you've devoted to your athletic career. I also understand the weird mental struggle you're wrestling with as you search for a new identity outside the realm of athletics.

I'm sure if you've picked up this book, you can remember your last day of competition similarly. I'm sure you can remember the feelings of needing that thing that motivates and gives you the same inspiration athletics did. I'm also very sure that you can remember the feelings of depression, confusion, and pure emptiness that can only be described as, being lost in your pursuit of something new. The old saying is, "... athletes die two deaths." This refers to the first death being the realization that a significant part of our lives and identity, which was in sports, is permanently over. The second is the obvious physical death to the grave.

This book will only focus on the former death and the methods I rediscovered to mold a new passion. I will explain how I utilize the tools and lessons gained from my lifetime of sports to push me into a new life and identity. We will dive into various topics that are geared towards helping you understand what you may be experiencing while also teaching you how to channel your experience from athletics then translate it to your new life. Through following the steps outlined in this book, I've been able to find renewed motivation and drive, which has pushed me to several fields where I'm achieving and working towards success. As of now, I'm the CEO of Martin Etiquettes LLC, a Soldier in the Georgia Army National Guard, a Minister, and now an author. I honestly hope this book helps motivate

Life After The Field

you to act and regain that same drive you had when you first found your thirst for athletics.

"Never lose sight of this important truth, that no one can be truly great until he has gained a knowledge of himself, a knowledge which can only be acquired by occasional retirement."
-Johann Georg Von Zimmermann

Life After The Field

Chapter 2: An Explanation to Consider

"...about 39% of athletes plan for life after competitive athletics while 26% of athletes give no thought to life post organized athletics. They also found that 56% of former athletes reported experiencing feelings of underachievement during the sport retirement phase"

-Brandy Sue Leffler

Life After The Field

This chapter is solely used to explain the mental shift you're going through. My explanation of these mental events aren't universal to everyone's mindset but rather an argument I've developed through personal experience and research. To put it plainly, my explanation may or may not apply to you. I do feel that getting an understanding of what the dilemma is mentally will help you to attain a sense of direction. You'll never know where to start if you never figure out where you're currently at. Before diving into all the techniques of establishing your new reality outside of sports, you must first deal with the current mental condition you're in.

First thing first, let's undo the stigma surrounding this matter. You're not weird or weak for feeling a sense of depression towards your athletic career ending. You're not spoiled for missing the life you experienced due to your athletic talent and hard work. There is no trophy or award for hiding the truth from yourself about how you feel. Being honest about your feelings towards this life transition is the first step to getting through it. There is a shroud of silence around this matter for athletes due to the nature of sports being a leisure activity that many outside of sports view as nothing more than child's play. Although this may be true when you consider the revenue generated from these sports, the level of attention and pressure thrown on athletes from adolescence all the way to the professional level, the sports world is nothing close to childish. The number of resources pumped into sports on an annual basis is astronomical. It's almost hilarious when we remember that boiled down to its roots, all sports are generally entertainment for children. When you think of all the factors that go into sports worldwide, you begin to see that there is a whole other world that's been developed around these children's games.

Being involved in this world as an athlete and achieving the praise, attention, and camaraderie that comes with success in sports creates a persona within this world that is also used to navigate the world outside of sports. As an athlete, you're viewed with a different perception by society, whether it's good or bad. From the time you begin your athletic career to its end, this persona is a part of how you identify; the longer your career, the more attached you become. Considering most athletes play sports most of their lives leading to their retirement, it makes perfect

Life After The Field

sense why there is a feeling of loss when the end arrives.

Once retirement is reached, you're taken out of this world you've known for so long and are now made to adjust to a life without access to a segment of life you're accustomed to escaping to for relief, decompression, and mental release. Without proper preparation, learning to cope outside of this world can be difficult. Retirement age for most collegiate athletes is typically around the early twenties, but this is an experience most people won't have until they are of retirement age of the late fifties to sixties. There are many changes happening to your world in your twenties, so dealing with your lost identity as well is a matter that requires your attention and understanding. Most young adults' maturity level isn't completely developed to deal with so many drastic life changes all at one time healthily, so seeking guidance and help on this matter will help more than it will harm. The more you neglect any hard feelings behind transitioning, the more you will wander aimlessly looking for the next thing to match up, only to be disappointed. If you don't get anything else from this chapter, remember that your feelings towards this life changing event are not an odd

Life After The Field

phenomenon. Most athletes admit to dealing with emotions of depression and anxiety post-retirement whether they have actively planned for it or not. To heal yourself and prepare for the transition, you must understand that this is normal and release the stigma of voicing your honest feelings and allowing yourself to dive into your mind to unpack your confusion.

The depression you may be feeling can be due primarily to the loss of identity. This book defines identity as the characteristics determining who or what a person or thing is. For most of your life, sports have been a crucial element to identifying yourself in the world. That's not to say that it's the only aspect of who you are, but it does play into how you identify, nonetheless. The realization of this identity being gone can cause a multitude of reactions as coping mechanisms. Unfortunately, some mechanisms are not as healthy as others and can create long term mental and physical damage to yourself and others. The key is to not look at this identity leaving as an eternal end but the beginning of a brand-new identity in another field. While some former athletes may be gifted with the talents to coach, allowing them to remain in their sport in a different

Life After The Field

capacity. Most of us will find ourselves learning to excel in another avenue completely different from the world of sports.

I personally think understanding that the path of highly competitive athletics has ended is a crucial step to progressing forward. The one fault of elite athletes is our obsession to never quit and our ability of continuous perseverance even in the face of incredibly unfavorable odds. This way of thinking can be a gift when pushing through hard times but can quickly become a curse in terms of not allowing parts of ourselves to change and transform to better serve our success. Use discernment in your journey of understanding. Are you hesitant to let your sport go because there is a true passion there, or are you simply lost for what you would do without it? Making peace with the end rather than constantly fighting it will bring you closure and create the mental space you require to find something new. When I retired from track & field, I dove into other competitive sports that I felt would scratch the itch. I tried CrossFit, Ninja Warrior, and many outlets that involved training and competition. Unfortunately, no other sport measured up to the love I had for track & field. It wasn't until I truly let go of that side of myself that

Life After The Field

I could completely move into a new passion. This process is certainly easier said than done, but this is no unknown territory for athletes. The purpose of this process of letting go is to create space in your mind to give thought to the many new ways you can transform yourself, build a new persona and apply your skills gained from sports to new markets.

"Preparation for old age should begin not later than one's teens. A life which is empty of purpose until 65 will not suddenly become filled on retirement."

-Dwight L. Moody

Life After The Field

Chapter 3: Finding the New You

"If you look good, you feel good, If you feel good, you play good, If you play good, they pay good."
-Deion Sanders

Life After The Field

An unfortunate side effect of losing your identity is a lack of motivation from a fitness perspective. Your main drive for being in top physical condition was to perform at the highest level. You always had a clear and defined competitor you could train to outperform, whether it be a rival team, the next opponent, or yourself. There was also a defined timeline that dictated a deadline you had to be ready to perform, which was a constant motivational force to train. That same timeline also allocated specific times every day for practice, weights or competition. With all those institutions of motivation now being gone, I found it difficult to do any physical activity due to there being no track meet to prepare for. I would constantly think to myself, "What is even the purpose of working out anymore? Why should I continue to push the limits of my body when there is nothing I'm preparing for?" These thoughts eventually wore me down and caused my desire for physical activity to slowly fade.

As I drifted into my funk, the lack of exercise took a toll on my physical appearance. The lack of exercise caused a lack of appetite due to my body being wired to consume the most food either before or after physical activity. I began to lose a

Life After The Field

significant amount of the muscle I'd built over the years, which, as you can expect, changed my body and transformed me into someone I didn't recognize. I'd easily slipped into my own state of depression whether I wanted to admit it or not. I had a lack of enthusiasm towards anything other than being stuck to video games. I didn't want to do any physical activity. I was lost mentally and had no sense of drive. This didn't fare the best for my life overall. With a new marriage that needed constant attention due to multiple constraints, a loss of personal conviction to push me in life, and the regret of past opportunities or lack thereof, it was the perfect storm for me to shut down and throw my own pity party.

    The weird thing about depression is, at times, the feeling creates a sense of happy complacency that births a cycle of wasted time and zero productivity. It's so easy to sink into that vacuum and become satisfied with the minimum while feeling a consistent sense of accomplishment based on your past victories. You validate your current position of doing nothing with the valor achieved from the days when you were once doing great things. But as the old saying goes, "Success is not owned, it is rented, and rent is due every day".

Life After The Field

A part of moving to the new you is understanding that those great things you did in the sports world don't give you a free pass to slack off today. After I graduated from high school, I was a state champion in two events. Although this was a major accomplishment, it wouldn't grant me success in the collegiate circuit. I had to work to a new level to excel; I couldn't depend on my past success to carry me to new heights. If you plan to continue to achieve great things, you must consistently push yourself and keep moving, whether things are good or bad. Steve Harvey once said, "if you going through hell, keep going. Why would you stop in hell?" This quote resonated with me and continues to push me to keep battling through the depression, confusion, and anger to this day. This serves as a constant reminder that a bad situation doesn't get better by ignoring it nor will it improve by always quitting or taking the easy way out. No one is coming to save you from yourself. Even if they wanted to, they couldn't. You must decide for yourself to get up and take actions to progress forward in life. It's not easy moving through the unknown, but I guarantee you it's much better than staying in the same place.

Life After The Field

It's somewhat obvious, but our outward appearance tends to play a big role in interacting with those around us. When we look good in a fashion we deem acceptable, we tend to display more confidence, take more risks, give off more positive energy, we adopt a more extroverted personality, and will more than likely have a higher percentage of success at whatever task is presented. On the flip side of this coin, we tend to take the opposite approach when we aren't displaying our best appearance. We're shyer, we take a more reserved introverted personality, we give off less inviting energy, and we feel less motivated to pursue tasks that may seem challenging. I'm not saying that looks mean everything but what I want to get across is that it does play a part in our day-to-day activities and personal psychology.

For example, let's say you're out and you see someone who you'd like to approach and ask on a date, but you didn't dress the best on the way out, and you're not completely comfortable with where your body stands from a physique point of view. You'll probably approach this interaction and give off energy that makes your prospective date lose confidence in your ability to be a suitable match and ultimately fumble this opportunity. They

Life After The Field

honestly don't have much confidence that you even think you deserve to go out with them based on how you chose to present yourself physically and from the social cues you display. Now let's rewind and say you saw this same person, but you dressed well based on the location where you met, and you've been exercising regularly, so you're satisfied with how your physique presents. This well-dressed, confident avatar of yourself may be the exact same person as the one with the low confidence and "I don't care" attire, but nine times out of ten will always obtain a more desirable outcome because it presents a better version of you.

Your motivation for staying fit and in shape may shift after retirement due to your athletic structure shifting. What I learned that helped me was channeling that same motivation I had to be one of the best at my college and use that to be the best version of myself for my wife, family, and country. This motivator keeps me focused and gets me up in the morning to get my workout in before I start my day. Your motivation may not be the same as mine, but I can promise you that whatever field you move to, staying in shape will help you from a mental and physical perspective. Your consistency of staying active while you were an athlete provided you many advantages over your peers that you may not have realized. Generally, regularly working out has been proven to do the following:

- Decreases Stress
- Provides Better Sleep
- Boosts Brainpower
- Increases Self Esteem
- Helps with depression and anxiety
- Reduces the chance of heart disease and cancer
- Provides more mood-enhancing chemicals such as norepinephrine, dopamine, and serotonin
- Makes you look sexy (I added this one)

These and many more were benefits you were taking full advantage of on a regular basis, but you may have never paid any attention to it. With your athletic outlet gone, this may be another explanation for why you're out of alignment mentally as well. There are so many important reasons to stay active, but I hope you find your motivation for getting back to the weight room, going to the court, running the trail, or whatever it is you do to stay active. Your future success in life

Life After The Field

depends on you keeping yourself healthy and looking as good as possible. Remember you're not training for top-level competition anymore; go easy on yourself. You don't have to bench 400 lbs., squat 700 lbs., and run a 4-minute mile. Just take care of your body, stay fit and eat well. There is no dire need to hit the weight room every day. If you miss a day here and there, don't beat yourself up. In sports, most people refer to it as having a short memory. Don't get so hung up on a negative event that it affects the future events to come. In my sports career, I found this to be an essential tool to playing my best. I found that if I made a mistake and focused on that one bad decision, I'd end up changing my game not to make that mistake again instead of playing to win. This doesn't sound bad but playing to win and playing not to make mistakes are two completely different things as many athletes know. You'll find that as you continuously play not to make an error, you'll find yourself neglecting other parts of your game and making more errors in the process. Where if I played to win and treated every play like a new day, I'd eventually do much better and, in some cases, exceed my expectations. I'd forget I even made a mistake in the first place. If you mess up one day, leave it in the past and move to the next with confidence, knowing you will do better. Create a schedule for yourself that will allow you to exercise and get yourself on track. I personally do 3 days a week for 45 minutes per workout. I may move to 4 if I'm feeling special. This schedule works for me and allows me plenty of time to get in a good workout, maintain a good-looking physique, and feel great.

Lastly, don't forget to also maintain a healthy diet. As you begin to get older, you'll see that your old college meal plan won't suffice to build a healthy body. Replace fast foods with grocery shopping. Add more vegetables and fruits to your plate. Drink water regularly, and remember you are what you eat. The demanding nature of athletics makes you conscious of the importance of diet, but it may not have been as important for some. For me, it wasn't a huge factor because I would burn so many calories during a day that if I was eating decent food, I was fine with some late-night fast food or snacks. Now that I'm older, I can certainly feel a difference in how certain foods influence aspects of my life. Eating well can be the difference between my getting up early or sleeping

Life After The Field

through my alarm. It plays a part in how good my morning workout goes and can determine how effective I am at my work. Food fuels your body in many ways that become more and more relevant the older you are. You can completely flourish or destroy your body solely based on the food options you choose daily, so pay attention.

"He who conquers himself is the mightiest warrior."

-Confucius

Life After The Field

Chapter 4: The Search for New Passion

"You must have a level of discontent to feel the urge to want to grow."
                                    -Idowu Koyenikan

Life After The Field

In the "adulting" phase of life (20 - 30 years old), we can quickly become burdened by the sheer weight of undertaking all or most the responsibilities our parents once did. I for one, was no exception to this reality. So, I did what any brand-new college graduate would do, I worked at the first place that would hire me to get some cash to figure this adulting thing out. Fortunately for me, I'd already been interning at a company in town for a year, so they hired me full time after finishing college. The job was good and paid well. It allowed me the income I needed to build a foundation to stand on and enough disposable income to spoil my girlfriend (now wife) occasionally. The job was in retail sales and wasn't too demanding, nor was it time-consuming. Everything seemed perfect except for one thing. I didn't like my job. In fact, eventually, I grew to hate this job. Through working there, I would convince myself that it was a great job and how fortunate I was to have found it. I tried every method I knew to inspire motivation in myself to stay. I eventually would go on to work there 3 years before finally quitting.

Next, I moved to a career in finance, which was more in line with my bachelor's degree in financial economics. I was convinced that this would, in fact, bring me the fulfillment I was looking for. After that new job glow wore off, I quickly found myself in the same position I did with my first job. A day-to-day routine where I would aimlessly complete tasks that brought me no sense of accomplishment or challenge. I'd work all day to reach goals that were of no particular interest to me. This realization frustrated me constantly. I'd gone through the trouble of switching fields and throwing away a promising career for one I thought would give me the fulfillment I was searching for, only to be disappointed.

Looking back on my work experience I looked to understand how my taste had soured overtime for jobs that both seemed to give me everything I could've wanted. Management was great, I'd worked multiple locations and even promoted, so what was the issue? I discovered that the foundation of my discontent was that ultimately, I had a lack of passion. I didn't particularly care about the jobs I just did them for the money or because they aligned with my major in college. While money is an understandable motivation for survival, it won't pass for the purposes of fulfillment in life. Although aligning with my major may have made me feel as though I was now taking advantage of my college education, it never motivated me to get out the bed or excited me to work overtime to achieve more. This isn't a message for you to quit your job to follow your passion but more so a clue to help you uncover things about yourself you may not know or have thought about. Think back to when you first started sports. You were motivated by the competition, the adrenaline, the pure enjoyment of just playing, and nothing more. When the game ended, no one owed you anything, and you weren't looking for anyone to give you anything for your participation. You simply enjoyed what you did out of intrigue for the sport. You didn't need a boost to get up to get ready for a game; you were excited to go. At your best, you didn't mind working harder than you ever had in your life to reach the next level. In life, this need for fulfillment and motivation doesn't change. Without true passion, that same drive won't come. Sure, you can fake it, but deep down, you'll know it isn't there.

The first step to establishing a new you is discovering a new passion in life. I wish this element to life was simple, but it's one that's much easier said than done. This process may be particularly hard as a former athlete because your passion was your sport, and now you must start over with a new area of interest and find fulfillment. My personal experience wasn't horrible due to revisiting an old interest I'd had, but my experience won't be the same for most. Learning new things and pursuing new goals can often be fun, depending on your perspective. I'm sure you would like to wake up tomorrow and have all the answers of where to go next, and I wish I could tell you but what I can give you are some tips to getting there faster.

1. Keep an open mind.

You'll never find something new with the same mindset. Your new passion could be anything and everything. Don't stifle your potential based on expectations made by those around you. Sometimes our biggest enemies can be those that mean well but don't understand who we truly are or where we want to go. You're not the same person today as you were last year, 5 years ago or when you were a child. Don't take advice from people who don't clearly understand where you are in life. Find space within yourself to decide who you want to be and where you want to go instead of constantly stressing about what people will think or say about your choices.

2. If you never had to work again, what would you do?

When I started looking for my new passion, this was a question I would often go back to in order to create perspective. What this question does is remove the major exterior motivating force of money and allows you to truly deep dive and reveal what you genuinely enjoy doing. Even if you can't think of an answer to this question, it provides you with an answer. If anything, it reveals that you have no force outside of monetary means to drive yourself. This isn't a good or bad thing, but it means you may want to investigate some subjects that may interest you to find an answer. If you want to take it a step further, if you can't find an answer think about what you spend your money on, and that can reveal where your true interests align as well. For most people, it's not money that they truly want; it's the things they can buy with money.

Life After The Field

3. What are some skills you have but haven't really developed?

I want you to sit down and think to yourself of all the things you've done in the past. I want you to think of old hobbies, interests, and things you've always been curious about. These topics may hide the clues to what you're looking for. For example, I found a passion for sewing clothes through an old interest in working with my hands as a kid. Sports had consumed so much of my life that I had neglected those parts of myself and almost forgot they existed. By going back and giving that interest a second chance, I've been able to start my own business and discover a lifelong talent that I can do virtually the rest of my life.

    I hope these tips were practical and useful for helping you discover that new passion to pursue. Remember, there is no race to this destination. There is no time limit, nor are there limits to when you can get started on this journey. The key is just to get started!

"My mission in life is not merely to survive, but to thrive; and to do so with some passion, some compassion, some humor, and some style."

-Maya Angelou

Life After The Field

Chapter 5: Learning The Basics

"I've failed over and over again in my life. And that is why I succeed."

–Michael Jordan

Life After The Field

Think back to your very first practice. I'm not talking about high school or college. Go all the way back to your little league days or however far back you can go. For most, these memories may bring up that nostalgia of the past and those great memories of your sport, but that's not what I want to focus on. I want you to think about the level of skill and proficiency you started at. Remember not being so good? Remember practicing for hours on end just to perfect a skill? Remember the thrill of accomplishment you experienced once you achieved your mastery of a skill? Remember the multiple failures, losses, bumps, and bruises along the way? There were some aspects to this growing stage that was fun, but for the most part, I'm sure you were ready for it to be over as soon as possible. The unfortunate reality about finding a new passion is that, just like when you were that little kid on the playground with no experience, skill, or expertise. You will have to restart and build from the ground up all over again.

To be excellent in your new field, you will have to go learn the basics first, just as you did as a rookie. In track, novice sprinters only train in athletic shoes until they've been properly taught running form, then track spikes are introduced. In

Life After The Field

football, new players aren't allowed to physically hit one another until they can demonstrate they have the proper technique for executing a tackle. In baseball, you literally start by learning to hit a ball off what's called a "tee" before you can square up to swing at a pitch. You will need to first dedicate yourself to learning the basics first before speeding to more advanced work in your respective fields. Don't forget you start with the basics to prepare a proper foundation for the more advanced techniques. You must be patient with yourself and remember that this is something new. You've started a new journey that can be a major success or failure, depending on how you prepare. Take the time to learn what you're doing, and don't rush to the front only to create a situation where you're way out of your league.

The problem with learning the basics of anything is that it's a very humbling experience. Especially when we're talking about a transition where you go from being a complete expert in your craft to now becoming a total novice with no idea of what you're doing. You're thrust back into the uncomfortable world of figuring things out and facing that repetitive process of trial and error. Patience is one of the most important keys to

Life After The Field

successfully navigating this phase. The biggest mistake people make when learning a new skill is most often in this development stage. We get so rushed to excel in something in the same manner we did in sports, that we don't take the time to consider how long it took us to reach the elite level. It took me seven years of work to be a consistent elite sprinter. It was nonstop, consistent progress that built me to a level of superior skill. It doesn't mean that being exceptional at another skill will take as long, but it puts in perspective that you truly can't rush greatness. Unfortunately, when you mix this pressure for immediate success with the influence of social media "flex" culture, you end up with a bunch of people with half-baked skills flaunting nothing more than mediocre results at best. The mediocrity eventually fails, but instead of failing privately where you can escape any embarrassment or shame, it's more than likely on the internet for full display. This failure isn't due to a lack of skill or potential but an inability to patiently learn and really understand what you're doing and what you truly want to achieve. Give yourself the space to mess up, correct, and mess up again. You wouldn't step on the field after one week of practice or even a month so treat your new gifts and skills the same way. Hone your talents, study the craft and fine tune yourself before you go presenting everything for criticism.

When I was first learning to sew, it took me quite some time to truly become good at what I do. I spent two years learning and perfecting my sewing skills and techniques. This required many late nights and early mornings of trial and error where I would work and not see anything remotely close to the progress I desired. As I kept working, I made many mistakes, and although at the time it was demoralizing, over time, it made me very skilled at my craft. By making mistakes, you learn how to fix them. By fixing errors, you get to see the real details of where you may have gone wrong and invent ways to avoid those pitfalls in the future. The errors that initially took me an hour or two to figure out, today, only take a matter of minutes to solve. My point is, I wouldn't be anywhere near as skilled as I am now if not for the multiple errors that taught me along the way. In the Army, there's a phrase we use called "embrace the suck." This phrase simply means that once you learn to mentally accept that a task may not be easy and will take a large amount of effort, completing the goal is much easier. This works well primarily because once you've reached acceptance in your

Life After The Field

mind, you can now shift all your mental capacity to the task at hand rather than sulking on how difficult the task may be. Mentally you can play a lot of tricks on yourself by shifting your mindset. If you approach difficult tasks with the idea that it's impossible and that you'll eventually fail, you most likely always will.

If you approach tasks with the mindset of "This is hard, but I'll get through and be better for it." Your results will trend more towards success. I spent two years working before I saw the first sale at my shop. I'm not saying that developing your skill will require the same sacrifice, but I am saying that you should be prepared to work and put time into whatever you choose to do. Learning the basics entails embracing the suck in some cases, but once you're an expert at your craft, you will be very thankful that you endured and stuck through the sacrifices you made.

"You're never a loser until you quit trying."
-Mike Ditka

Life After The Field

Chapter 6: Mastering The Craft

"There may be people that have more talent than you, but there's no excuse for anyone to work harder than you do."

-Derek Jeter

Life After The Field

After you've learned the basics and are secure in the level of ability you've gained, it's time to start looking to for more advanced levels of improving your skills. Mastery is defined as the possession or display of great skill or technique. Although being a master at something isn't necessary for a degree of success and fulfillment, it does offer an extra layer of value in the realm of separating yourself from the crowd and discovering your best self. When I left athletics, I was somewhat relieved because I thought the demanding nature of sports and the pressures to perform and excel were forever a thing of the past. I knew the cost for excellence in sports, and I willingly paid the price with my body, time, and effort. In return, I received high athletic achievement and a distinguished career. I was foolish in thinking that because my physically demanding pursuits had ended that the price of high work ethic and the stress of rising to the occasion would also diminish.

In the world outside of sports, life is blunt but not as strikingly hurtful as the world of sports. For example, if I wanted to live my life and only put forth the minimum effort and only do safe and easy things, I could probably live a relatively decent life.

Life After The Field

I would possibly find a wife who would accept this watered-down version of myself. I could find a job that would cater to my desire to only do the minimum. Bring home an average salary, live within my limits, occasionally indulge in a few luxuries, and have a relatively good life. Obviously, this life is not one where I'm making the best use of my talents and abilities, but it still allows me a degree of success and pleasure. In the world of sports, the minimum almost always leads to crushing defeat. Your mediocrity and shortcomings are put on full display as your opponent dominates you mercilessly. There is no reward or consolation prize for losing, regardless of the excuse. This stark punishment for being unprepared is a direct driving force for many to perform to excellence and experience the amazing rush of a victory.

With the modern-day progression of the corporate workspace, there really isn't such a black and white, win-loss dynamic to work. Competition is barely existent at best, and even in instances where there is competition, the rewards for excelling is not worth the effort given. This reality lulls most into a sense of complacency where you become satisfied with simply getting through the

Life After The Field

day instead of striving to be the best at whatever you do. The problem with this mentality is that we are blinded by the illusion of comfort while the game of wins and losses constantly takes place around us daily. If you're blind to the game, I can guarantee that you're on the losing side. While you're comfortable, someone is getting promoted for going the extra mile, someone is using their passion to create a million-dollar company, someone is meticulously paying off massive amounts of debt, someone is establishing a whole new life for generations to come. These accomplishments aren't on a stadium screen where you can slowly track their progress; they're happening every day behind closed doors. Those people decided to constantly push themselves and set goals to conquer. They didn't allow themselves to get lost in the sauce of the mundane day to day. They developed a plan, stayed focused, and executed with merciless precision. I'm not saying that you're losing to these people, but what I am saying is that these people could easily be you. You just haven't decided to pursue anything more than the minimum of what's required to get by. These individuals understood the price of what it would cost to achieve their goals and paid the price to achieve them. While sports clearly define a winner and loser, life outside of sports demands that you create your own standard for what a win or loss is. You must know what it takes for you to get better and monitor whether you've improved (won) or become worse (lost).

One of my coaches always said, "You're either getting better or worse, but you never stay the same." This approach to life is crucial to progressing towards your goals daily. The previous two paragraphs serve to set the foundation for establishing the idea that mastery of your passion or craft may not be necessary but is essential to winning daily. Let me be clear I don't consider myself a master at what I do yet. I continue to improve and seek knowledge because I know that fine-tuning my skills and pushing the limits of my abilities will transform me into a better business owner and improve the value of my creations, which will improve my business's value. Becoming a master clothier is a goal of mine that I'm confident I'll reach through my consistent work and growth. I also know that If I get stuck and complacent in my abilities now, I'll forfeit the chance to grow my business. Sports gave me clear fixed goals. Run faster today than I did yesterday, and I could literally know whether I'm better or worse based on

Life After The Field

the time I ran. Life is a little more complicated, but figuring out how to measure my success is still vital to progress. Whatever your passion, strive to be what you consider to be your absolute best. Become a master, push your limits, stay diligent and watch how your dreams unfold with great abundance.

"If you aren't going all the way, why go at all?"
-Joe Namath

Life After The Field

Chapter 7: The Devil Is in The Routine

"Without self-discipline, success is impossible, period."

-Lou Holtz

Life After The Field

The biggest problem I had with effectively transitioning to my new self was finding a new routine to adjust to. Through sports, there was structure and order to everything. Although this may not have been the most attractive aspect of sports, it was efficient in helping me train and perform. Now it was my responsibility to figure out how I could make the best of my time. Unfortunately, I immediately made the mistake of doing everything I wanted to do first, then prioritizing self-development and more difficult tasks afterward. As you can imagine, this created a vacuum of wasted time and procrastination where I either couldn't get myself unglued from video games, or I'd end up falling down a social media rabbit hole. Whatever the case, by the time I was done "having fun," I wouldn't have time to focus on more important tasks like getting in a workout or working on my business. My unproductive days would typically go in this fashion:

- Wake up in the morning with just enough time to shower and get dressed to go to work
- Work from 9 – 6pm

Life After The Field

- When I get home, I'd talk to my wife and get on the game or retreat to my phone from about 6:30 – 9ish
- Somewhere in this 6:30 – 9ish time, I'd eat dinner
- 9:30pm – whenever, I'd binge watch TV and may leave the comfort of leisure to do something productive
- When I would get off my butt, I'd decide between pulling out my sewing machine or working out for like 30 minutes.
- Then I'd go to sleep

This cycle would repeat itself for quite some time before I realized I wasn't getting anything done. I had too many distractions sucking away precious time. My problem was obvious. If I had goals I wanted to achieve, I needed to intentionally allocate my time towards my vision.

Although I wanted to start a business and regain my physical physique, it would not happen simply because I wanted it in my mind. I literally needed to create a plan to accomplish the task. Although I didn't enjoy the idea of having a planned schedule for my life, that's exactly what I did. Before I began planning a schedule, I needed

Life After The Field

to first identify and eliminate time-consuming distractions. As much as I loved video games, I had to come to the honest conclusion that the more time I put into playing, the less time was spent getting anything done. I was sacrificing my dreams and future for a game. At this point in my life, I wanted to make a change and decided to eliminate this factor, so I sold my system. Let me make myself clear, in no way am I saying that video games are bad. There are plenty of talented people who are uniquely gifted at video games and can make a living from cultivating those skills and talents. I'm just not one of those people. For me, I didn't have the proper amount of time to devote to video games, my goals, and priorities. I had to eliminate the things that didn't align with me reaching my goals, and video games just so happened to be one of those things. I can't tell you what is good or bad for your goal progression. I can't tell you how you should be allocating your time. What I can tell you is until you reach the goal you're dedicated to, you should do your best to eliminate things that distract you from achieving daily progress. Once you get to a point where you are content and happy with the progress you've made, you can once again devote more time to leisure, but until that day arrives, stay focused.

Life After The Field

Next was managing my phone. Social media can be a useful tool, and it can also become a useless one depending on how you use it. By going down endless rabbit holes on multiple social media platforms, I would waste time and utilize none of these platforms' benefits. I wouldn't learn anything, sell any products, or find interests that could be useful to me. I clearly needed to limit the amount of time spent stuck to a device.

I also needed to organize my priorities as well to better create a schedule of tasks. The love I have for my family will always be a priority, so making time for them is a non-negotiable factor. Nurturing my spiritual health is also an area I needed personal time for. Without the organization of my time and priorities, I would never be efficient in making progress towards my goals. Once these factors were aligned, I was able to begin making significant progress in my tasks. This method of organization and elimination was a real game-changer. By honestly evaluating my priorities and then eliminating the distractions that kept me away from reaching my goal created a laser-focused version of myself. My time was allocated properly while my actions were intentional and for a

Life After The Field

purpose. I effectively used every hour of the day to improve and progress towards my goals.

With the adjustments, my routine changed to this:

- 6-7am Wake up to meditate and work on my business
- 8:15 – 9am Get to work
- 9am – 6pm Work
- 6:30 – 7:15ish Workout
- 8– 9pm Dinner (Family Time)
- 9– 10ish Continued Family Time mixed with Business
- 10:30pm Sleep

This routine eliminated distractions and idle time vacuums while providing time to rebuild my physique and develop my business. It also created opportunities to focus on prioritizing spending time with my family and getting good quality sleep. Getting good sleep gave me an extra boost to wake up earlier and be productive with my morning. Getting up early in the morning is not a task that is uncommon to most athletes. It's typically the most convenient time when there are no distractions, and it's the perfect chance to focus on work with a clear mind. It's honestly a top tier life hack to being more productive with your day. Honestly, you've probably been doing this since your high school days. Don't stop! Keep getting up early, it's not easy, but an extra hour in your day can make a major difference in productivity. Waking up early gave me an extra hour and a half to dedicate to my business, which was a catalyst for me to grow faster. Achievement requires sacrifice, and I had to realize that I couldn't do everything I enjoyed while also accomplishing my goals all at the same time. One must take priority over the other. Once I surrendered to this idea, I was able to be productive with my goals while also maintaining my priorities. You're probably familiar with this form of discipline since it was in place all your life as an athlete. You've been given a blueprint for succeeding in virtually any field you choose. The practice wasn't fun, but you went every day to get better and eventually became exceptional at your sport. Workouts were hard, but you learned that the burn and pain were necessary to make you better. The same applies to your goals; you must find ways to work and exercise your gifts often. It's not easy working through exhaustion, depression, or doubt, but establishing a system to push through is necessary to reach your goal. You can do this! Make the changes today. Identify your

Life After The Field

distractions and eliminate them. Identify your priorities and values. Create a schedule that allows you to work and concentrate on your goal while also being able to nurture your priorities. The difference between your success or failure can most often be a result of your daily routine. Pay attention to where most of your time is going and look for ways to better use your time. Every day is a chance to improve and move closer to your goal, don't waste it.

"Hard work beats talent when talent doesn't work hard."

–Tim Notke

Life After The Field

Chapter 8: Diversify Your Skill Set

"You are unique. You have different talents and abilities. You don't have to always follow in the footsteps of others. And most important, you should always remind yourself that you don't have to do what everyone else is doing and have a responsibility to develop the talents you have been given."

-Roy T. Bennett

Life After The Field

I always loved watching exceptional athletes. No matter the sport, it was a pleasure being able to watch a true talent perform at an elite level. One thing that I recognized that was universal to any great athlete was that they all possessed multiple skill sets. If they wanted, these athletes could play multiple positions and perform at top tier levels at all of them. This section uses this concept and makes it practical to your growth outside of sports. To reach the next level in your journey to redefine self, you must be open to learning multiple skill sets. The fun part about discovering new skillsets is that it shows you a side of yourself that you never knew existed. Everything may not stick, but the things that do make you a better person all around. For example, in football, if you're a running back that's open to the idea of also running wide receiver routes you may discover an ability to catch as well. This opens an offense to more options and improves your overall value as a player. Keeping an open mind and trying new things can improve your overall value as an individual and team player. On the flip side of this example, if you're a running back and you're very hesitant or even resistant to running wide receiver routes, you ultimately limit the options an offense has and limit your overall value.

Life After The Field

So, through a closed mind, you hurt yourself and those working with you. Your mental ability to adapt is a characteristic that can provide high levels of success. It's a common factor shared between sports and the world outside of athletics. Your mindset can create clear pathways or complex obstacles.

You're more talented, creative, and innovative than you truly know. The catch is you must constantly try new things to uncover these many sides to your own brilliance. This process can be frustrating, time-consuming, and tedious, so here are a few tips that may spare you a headache:

- Avoid gimmicks. By a gimmick, I mean activities that don't necessarily help you cultivate any legitimate skills but allow you to ride a momentary wave creating the illusion of a skill set that really doesn't exist. Social media has created the illusion of success and skillfulness via the influencer platform. While some influencers truly do have skill sets and knowledge that create income streams for themselves, others may only be successful for reasons that aren't based on them having a special skill set or knowledge base. Success

Life After The Field

itself is not a problem, but maintaining that success will be. When you use gimmicks to build yourself, you leave no foundation to stand on outside of the momentum of the trend you're riding. Take the time to develop a skillset and build a knowledge base behind topics and areas that truly interest you. Knowledge is powerful; it can be distributed via any platform, it doesn't expire, nor does it lose value in repetition. The same goes for developed skills. Learn how to do something yourself that you can leverage and control at your will. I learned how to make clothes myself to start a company where I can do what I want, sell how I want, and control every piece of the process. My skills allow me leverage to control every step of my business. Essentially, I made myself the player, the referee, and the coach all at the same time, and you can do this too by cultivating skills and knowledge.

- Avoid money traps. This tip goes back to the chapter on finding your passion. Don't chase money when looking for your new interest. Especially in this generation of possibilities, anything you're interested in has a market and audience for it. Beware of the get rich quick companies and pyramid schemes that offer freedom but truly make you dependent on them in the long run for your success. To be more specific, don't get caught up in groups where all they talk about is how much money you can earn but, they aren't developing you and giving you the skills to be independent. A good way to know if what you're doing is helping or harming you is to ask yourself, "What am I learning? What skills are they teaching?" If you're left confused by these questions, you may be in the wrong place. Your time is valuable, and you should use it to make yourself better instead of growing everyone else's bottom line. Of course, you want your skills to be profitable, but you don't want your only motivation to be driven by money. This concept always seems crazy to those of us who aren't from backgrounds of the rich and wealthy, but it never fails that money doesn't bring fulfillment in the long term.

Learning multiple skills offers a sense of security as well. Although this book aims to help you move forward and excel in a new field, I never

Life After The Field

want to rule out the possibility that you may have many passions and gifts that you can exercise. It's a proven fact that the more positions you can play in any sport, the more valuable you are. The same applies to you and your skills. The more skills you know, the more control you have over how you want to use your abilities to benefit you. Remember, the initial problem was caused by focusing on sports and not really giving much attention to other options outside of that. Let's begin to undo that action by finding a passion and not getting consumed by it necessarily but using it as a vehicle to find other passions to build off. For example, I can use the profits I make from my sewing skill to invest in stocks or trade options. The profits from the investing skill I can use to learn about vending machines and start multiple businesses from that skill. Just from learning and developing, I can create three separate independent streams of income that I can control 100%. Knowledge and skills are powerful, and you have at least one skill, if not many, locked inside yourself, find one today!

"You have to expect things of yourself before you can do them."

-Michael Jordan

Life After The Field

Chapter 9: Mind Control

"Champions aren't made in the gyms. Champions are made from something they have deep inside them—a desire, a dream, a vision. They have to have the skill, and the will. But the will must be stronger than the skill."

-Muhammad Ali

Life After The Field

I think it goes without saying that taking care of your mental health is an important aspect of living a healthy life. The problem for most isn't understanding that we need a healthy mind but developing actions to cultivate positive mental growth. We do so many things habitually that have created an environment that stifles our capacity to improve on a mental level. We've mentioned the importance of mindset in previous chapters, but now we will dive into the fine details of cleaning up your mind and efficiently improving your mental health. When making the transition from sports to your new life, your mental health, in my opinion, is at its most vulnerable. With you reinventing your identity, there are so many influences that can steer you in a direction of where to go next. They also can cause you to believe things about yourself that aren't true. Be intentionally aware of the following factors: who you spend time with, your social media consumption, and how you're developing your mind.

You're the sum average of the five people you spend the most time with, so your relationships should always benefit you in some way. This may sound odd and selfish, but there is significant meaning behind taking inventory of your relationships and

Life After The Field

determining if they're a benefit or liability to your growth. There shouldn't be people in your life who consistently cost you time, energy, and effort but never reciprocate equally. You will always find yourself frequently exhausted and depleted rather than being reenergized and encouraged. The circle of friends you choose to spend time with, play such a big part in how you view the world, reality, and yourself that you can't afford to hang around those who only leave you doubtful, self-conscious, and unmotivated through interaction. Especially in a time of life where you're looking to move into a new identity and reestablish your passion. Be cautious of the following friends that can be costing you your mental health.

- The Competitor – This friend is deceptive but, if left unchecked, will cause unnecessary conflict and distraction in your life. This is the person who means well but never really can be your friend because they see your life as a competition to theirs. Any success you achieve they view as a signal of your superiority to them instead of just your individual success. They're the one who constantly has a story for everything you've done, but it's coincidentally always better than yours. They're always happy

Life After The Field

when you succeed in life but can never tolerate you "doing better than them". They will compliment your success but underscore it with their version of what they would do in your position or how they could've done better with your talents. With them, their projected insecurity is never blunt and obvious, but their demeanor is sprinkled with a distinctive sense of judgment and dissatisfaction with everything that doesn't serve their ego. This friend will create anxiety to constantly seek acceptance in your relationship. This will eventually deflect you from focusing on progressive growth to trying to win a back and forth with someone who wasn't meant to be in comparison to you.

- The Devil's Advocate- This friend will always claim to have good intentions as well but will always create mental obstacles in your pursuit of new horizons. I named this friend the Devil's Advocate mockingly, as you might imagine. Being the Devil's Advocate in a scenario is never a bad thing; it's actually wise, but this friend's problem is they will always play this role. They will always find the negative perspective of any scenario brought up. Their ultimate goal is to convince everyone that nothing is worth doing outside of their view of the world. They lack the drive to aspire for more for many reasons and are motivated to persuade others to sulk in their reality as well. Misery loves company, and this friend is always miserable and stuck, and unfortunately, you can't save them. The best way to help is to separate yourself from this relationship.

- The Forever Friend- This friend may be your best friend but also your worst enemy. The Forever Friend is the friend you've probably known for a long time, and you both share a special relationship. You all have been through everything together and have a wider breath of knowledge on each other than most. This knowledge of one another may be a fault of your relationship as you begin to transition to something new. When you begin to change in order to progress to something new, this can be seen as a "betrayal of self" to your peers. Everyone won't accept that you're ready to change and base their argument solely on the fact they've known you for a long time and believe you should remain the same person in order to maintain some false sense of loyalty to a part of yourself that is no longer to your benefit to hold on to. The argument isn't the problem but having peers who can't recognize that you're transforming for the better is. We value the opinions of those closest to us, so use discernment when embracing the opinions and mindsets of your friends. Some will keep you stagnant and halt your ability to move forward to new things. Some friends can't allow you to change due to them not being able to fathom you being anything other than what they've known you to be. While their concern is passionate and from a place of care, it's misplaced.

There are obviously so many more different types of people that can be a detriment to your transition, but I wanted to highlight a few that you may not have thought about. Just remember to watch the company you keep because they play a role in who you are, have been, and will become.

Social media is a wonderful tool that has revolutionized our world in ways that are unimaginable. We don't know the specific influences of social media consumption on the brain, but the effects on how it molds our sense of self-worth are evident. Studies have linked social media interaction to having addictive qualities through multiple small dopamine hits you receive through many of the most popular apps. In case you didn't know, dopamine is a chemical your brain produces that motivates actions through a feeling of happiness. This addictive chemical has become the crux behind many young adult's anxieties, impatience, and feelings of discontent with themselves. On your journey to rediscovery, I urge you to drastically limit your consumption of social media content that isn't educational to realizing your new passion. I advise this only because social media can easily reinforce the belief that you have to be a complete human being devoid of flaws and perfectly successful before your 30's. This false reality can cause people to retreat to whatever path will help them achieve the level of success social media has deemed the standard. They will get so caught up in chasing the illusion of success that they'll neglect the idea of following their own vision for what success looks like. The truth is no one ever truly has it all together, we're all just looking to do a little better every day, and the only people who are truly happy are the ones who decided to go against the grain and listen to themselves. Success is objective and is different for all of us. Find your own perspective for what success looks like before allowing social media to determine whether you're a success or failure based on a measurement of success you never aspired to achieve. Take some time to eliminate any content that's flashy, boastful, and unnecessary. Watch how the perspective of yourself and your life in general changes by simply monitoring what you feed your brain via social media intake.

Lastly, I want you to focus on what you're doing to develop your mind habitually. What are you listening to, reading, watching? The signals we take in daily have a great influence on how we view our world as well. As you begin to create a new world for yourself, don't forget to be aware of how you're building your mind. There are numerous methods you can take advantage of to boost mental stimulation. Find content that's motivational and will allow you to feel good about yourself. As you grow in a new direction, don't allow your self-esteem to falter due to your lack of current direction. You will constantly judge your life day by day, and at some points, trying to stay positive can be a struggle all by itself. It's important that you feed your mind as much optimistic data as possible. From the shows you watch, the

Life After The Field

podcasts you listen to, and the books you read, keep pushing positivity. Your mind is the strongest weapon to success you have. Great talent can't succeed with a weak mind.

"Happiness can be found even in the darkest of times if one only remembers to turn on the light."

-Albus Dumbledore

Life After The Field

Chapter 10: Execution

"In baseball and in business, there are three types of people. Those who make it happen, those who watch it happen, and those who wonder what happened."

-Tommy Lasorda

Life After The Field

Do you know what a "backwards K" means in baseball? In a scorebook a "K" denotes a strikeout for a batter but a "backwards K" denotes a strikeout where a batter did not swing at the pitch. This means that the batter literally watched a pitch from the mound to the plate and refused to take a swing. Outside of swinging and letting go of the bat, this is the most embarrassing occurrence in baseball! Striking out is typical considering a batter that gets on base 30% of the time or (.300) is hailed as exceptional. Striking out with a backwards k is a different story. It's humiliating because it implies you didn't even try to swing. Almost like giving up and going down without a fight. Whether the batter didn't swing because they doubted themselves or just gave up, it's an action that is frowned upon. Life works similarly in this fashion. We're given opportunities to excel or, like in this example, at-bats. We can choose to swing at the pitches thrown or take a "backwards K ". Please swing, in life, you only need one good opportunity to change everything, but you'll never get your shot if you never swing. Keep taking chances and putting yourself out there.

Nothing is sadder than seeing someone with all the potential in the world fail from a lack of confidence and action. We all know those who have planned and prepared for an eternity and never make their move. They say they'll start tomorrow, they say they will ask that person out next time, they say the timing isn't right, and they never end up getting anything done. They ultimately sit on a mountain of excuses for why something hasn't worked out or started. If you have made it to this point in the book, I hope you've taken away at least a few pieces of wisdom to propel you into the next phase of your life. Although this book itself won't be the cause for your newly discovered identity, I sure hope it's the catalyst that kicks you into gear. I hope I've ignited a flame in your being that inspires you to try something new and pursue things you'd never imagined. More than anything else, I hope that when it's time to make the final decision to act, you do it without hesitation. I want you to apply for that job knowing that you're prepared and ready. I want you to start that business you've thrown your heart into. I want you to live your life with the full intention of where you're going and how you plan to get there. So much of our lives are cut short by ourselves through doubt and concern. If I had started working on my business intentionally when I had the idea, Lord knows how far I'd be by now. Instead, I sat on my gift for years and neglected its possibility. I was afraid I'd fail. I

Life After The Field

thought learning to sew would be too difficult. I thought I couldn't start my business because it cost too much money to build. All those reasons were all invalid and nothing but excuses for me to hide behind. They made me feel good for not trying in the first place. The excuses insulated me from having to face myself and be accountable for not even giving myself a chance. I'd accomplished unimaginable feats in track and field but lost sight of everything I was capable of because I allowed my fear, doubt, and complacency to overshadow the unknown bounds of my abilities.

My message to you is to execute your passion. Execute your dream. Execute your goals. Be intentional about working towards what you say you want out of life. Don't say you want to change your weight but don't prepare a meal plan. Don't say you want to learn a new skill and never sacrifice to make time to learn. Don't claim you want the promotion but never put in the extra work. You can do the work. You can pass the tests. You can learn the skills. You can change your life. As the old saying goes, your only real competition is you. You have the work ethic to persevere. You know how to push yourself. This book is absolutely useless to you if you put it down and continue to

Life After The Field

do the exact same things you've always done. Walk into this next life the same way you stepped onto that field, grabbed those spikes, or walked onto the court, with the attitude of assured victory and dominance.

"You miss 100% of the shots you don't take."
- Wayne Gretzky

Life After The Field

A Letter To Former Athletes

Thanks so much for picking up this book and giving it a read. I wrote this book specifically to help those lost in transition and needing a guide to put them back on track. I wrote this book to tell you that you're not alone in your search to find life again. You're not the only athlete who is anxiously searching for how they can scratch that competitive itch. You're not the only one stuck and mentally depressed reflecting on the "old days" when life was simple, and you reigned supreme. I was literally in the exact same place but got out with the instructions outlined in this book. I poured so much of my heart into this work and reflected on all the times I'd been lost, confused, frustrated, and uncertain about everything. What I can tell you is things won't get better unless you get up and make them better. You must act. Your athletic career has gifted you with so many tools to succeed in just about any field there is in the world, but you must use them. Even if you hadn't planned for your sports retirement or were forced to retire, we all must stop playing eventually. When that end comes, it's merely the beginning of a brand-new adventure in another world. Except you're stronger, you have mental endurance, you're goal-oriented and a fighter. Move forward with the understanding that your sports life may be over, but you're entering the next stage of life with an advantage. Use it!

Life After The Field

About the Author

This section is just to give you a little insight into me. I'm from Tuscaloosa, Alabama, born August 4th, 1993. I come from an amazing family, raised by my parents, Tim & Portia Martin, who are the best educators this world has known. I have an older brother Tim Martin Jr. who has been my biggest supporter since I was born. My immediate family now consists of my lovely wife, Aspen Martin, and daughter, Noah Grace Martin. We currently live in Atlanta, Georgia. I want to leave my mark on this world and make someone's life better, as my parents have done for so many people. As educators, they can't count how many lives they've influenced and molded just through their example. This book is one of the many ways I plan to accomplish this goal. If you ask anyone who knows me, they will tell you I'm an easy-going person. A perfect day for me is a Saturday of watching college football while grilling some food on a warm evening of about 75 degrees with a slight wind. I'm an old soul in some regards, thanks to my distinct love of Motown classics and old school rock and roll. If you want to see more of my life or family, you can follow me on Instagram @TheBenMartin, @__TheMartins, or check out my business @MartinEtiquettes. I'm a friendly guy, if you have questions or want more information, DM me via Instagram or send me an email at @MartinEtiquettes@gmail.com.

www.ingramcontent.com/pod-product-compliance
Lightning Source LLC
Chambersburg PA
CBHW011142290426
44108CB00023B/2716